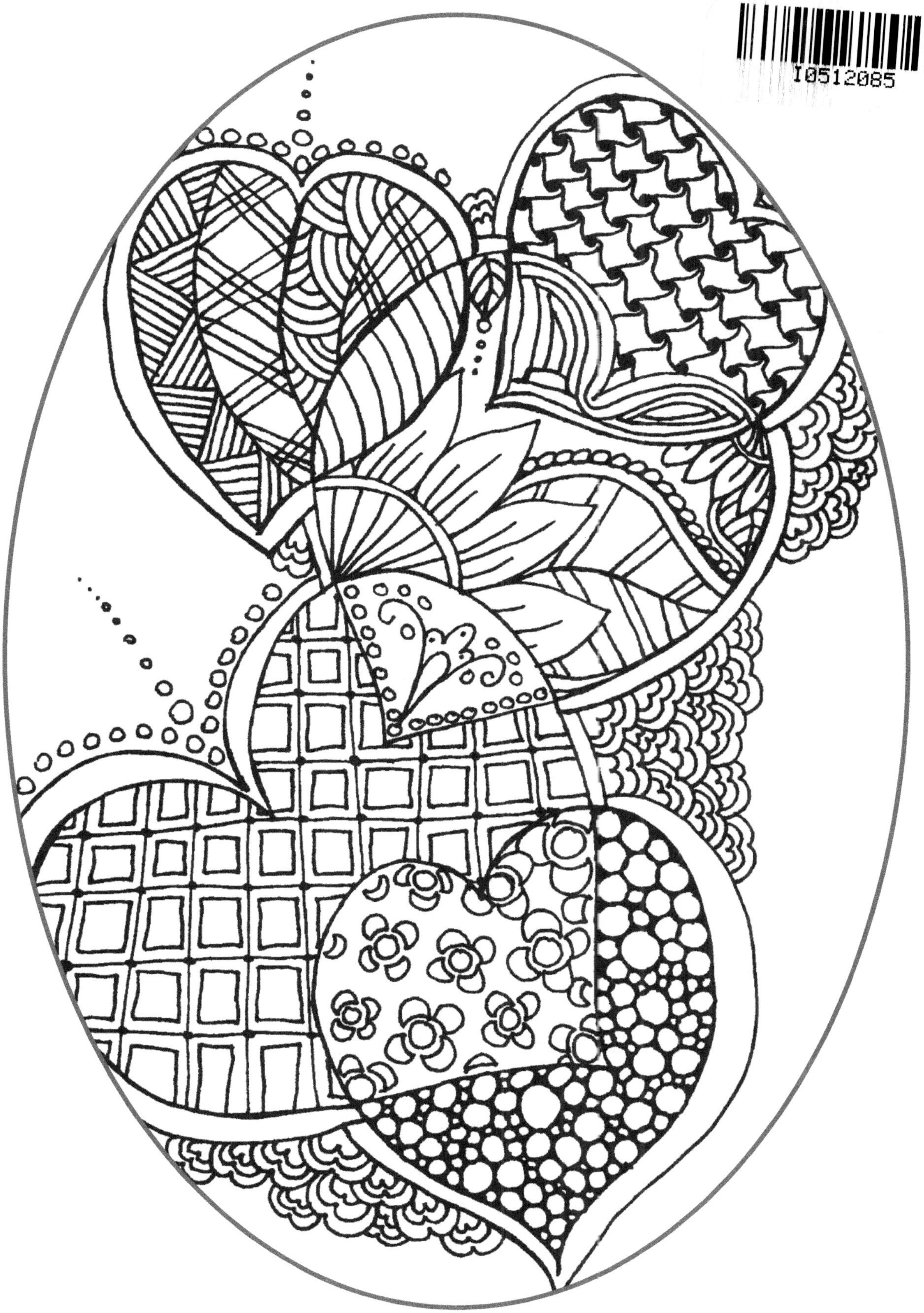

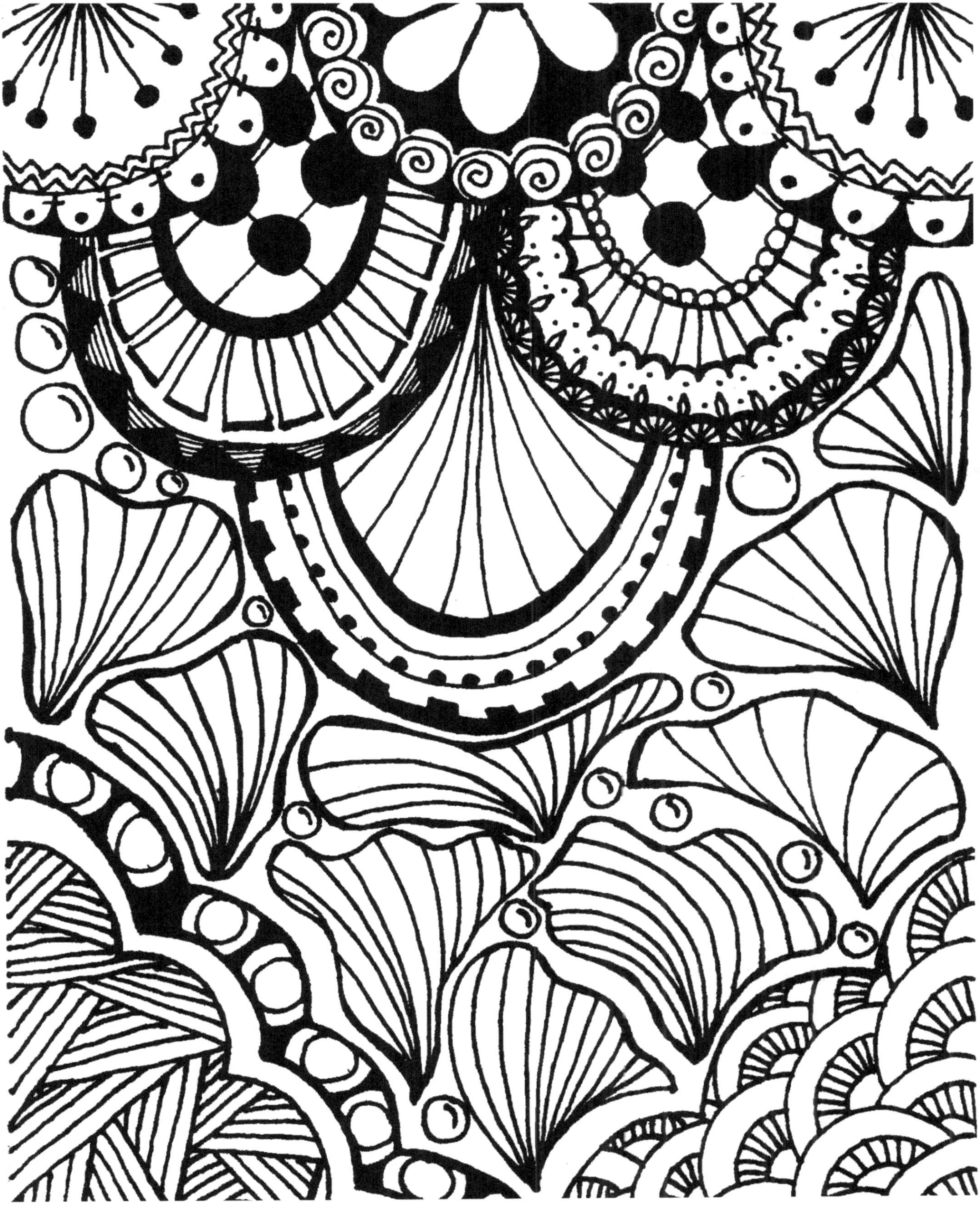

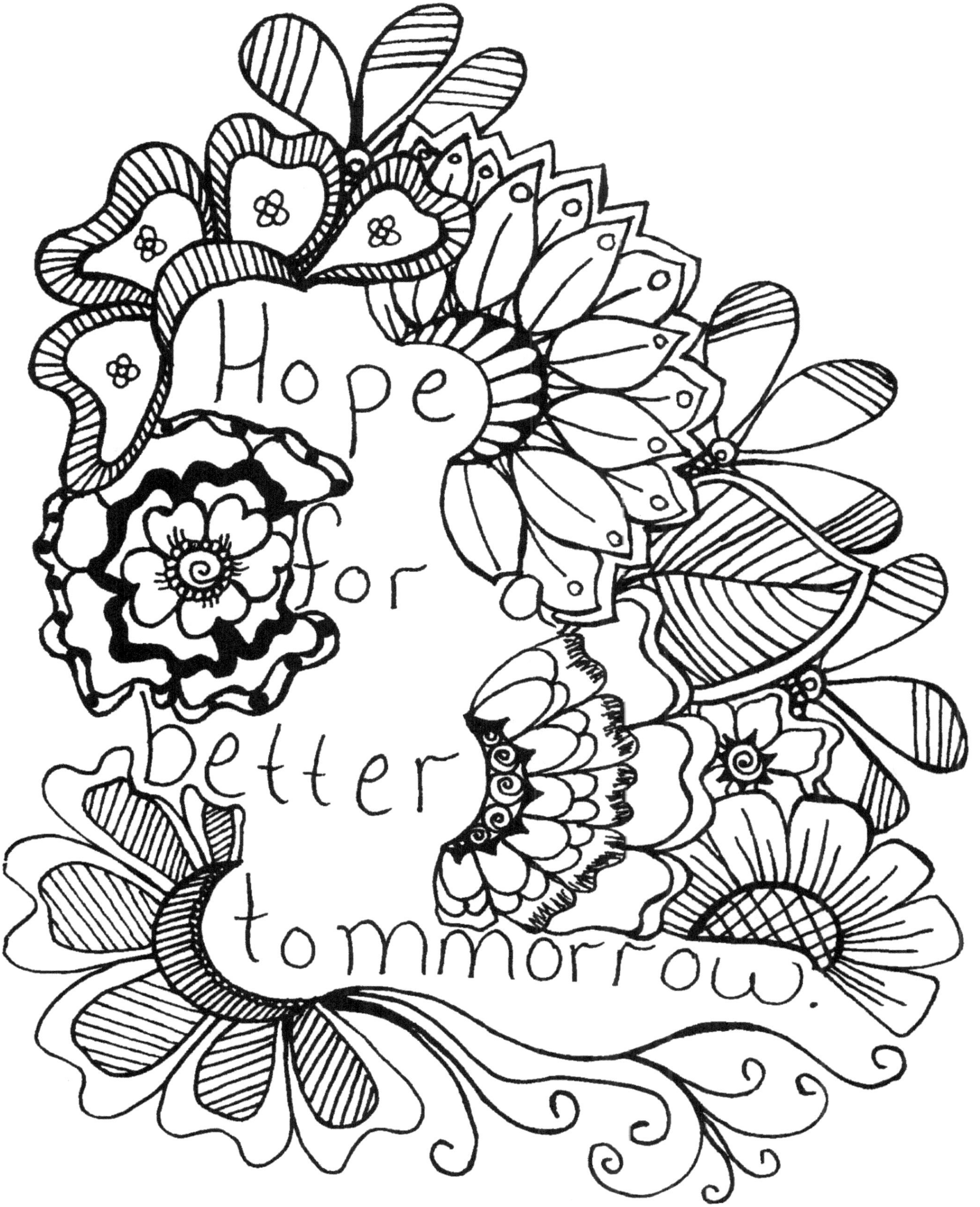
Hope
for a
better
tommorrow.

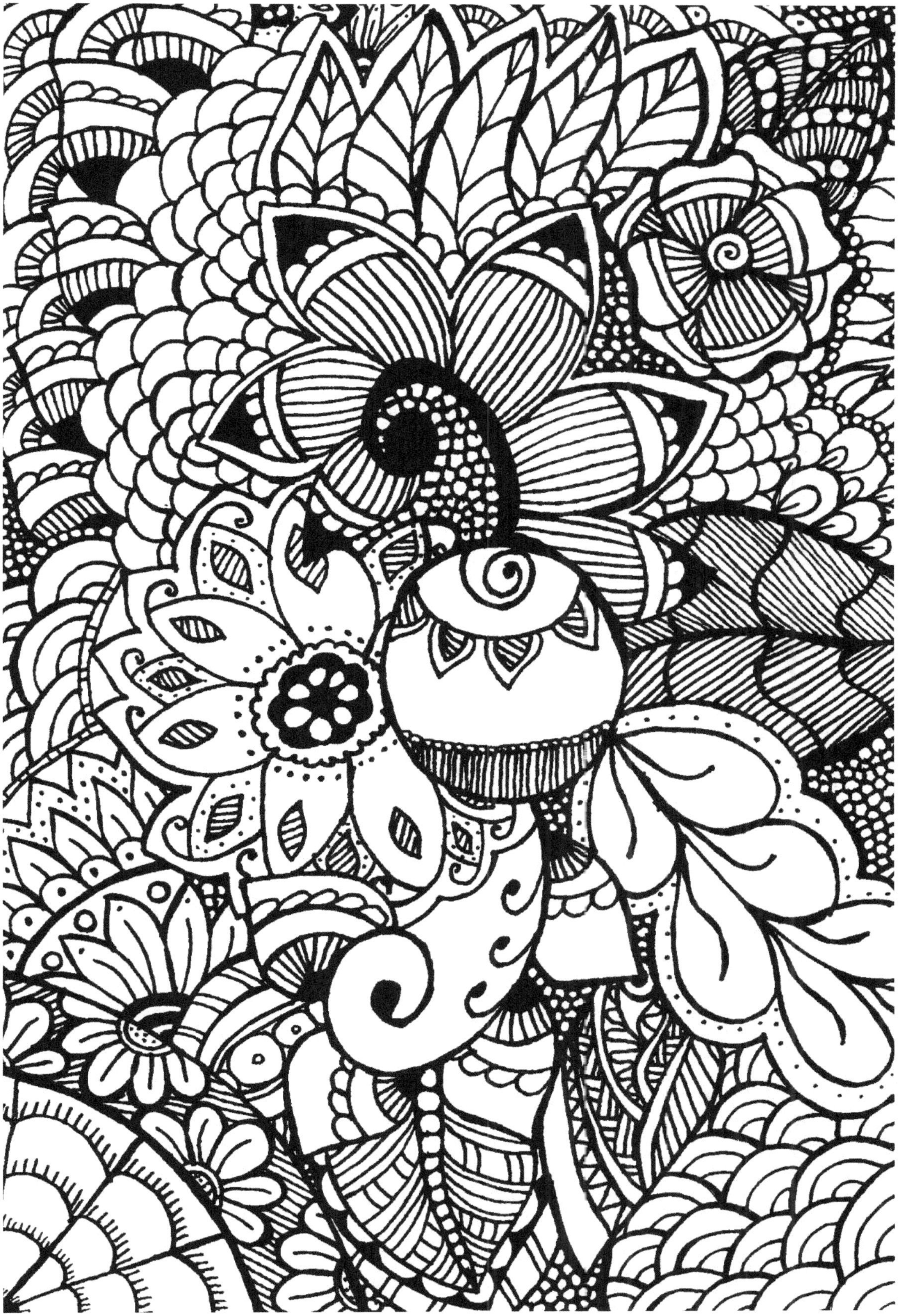

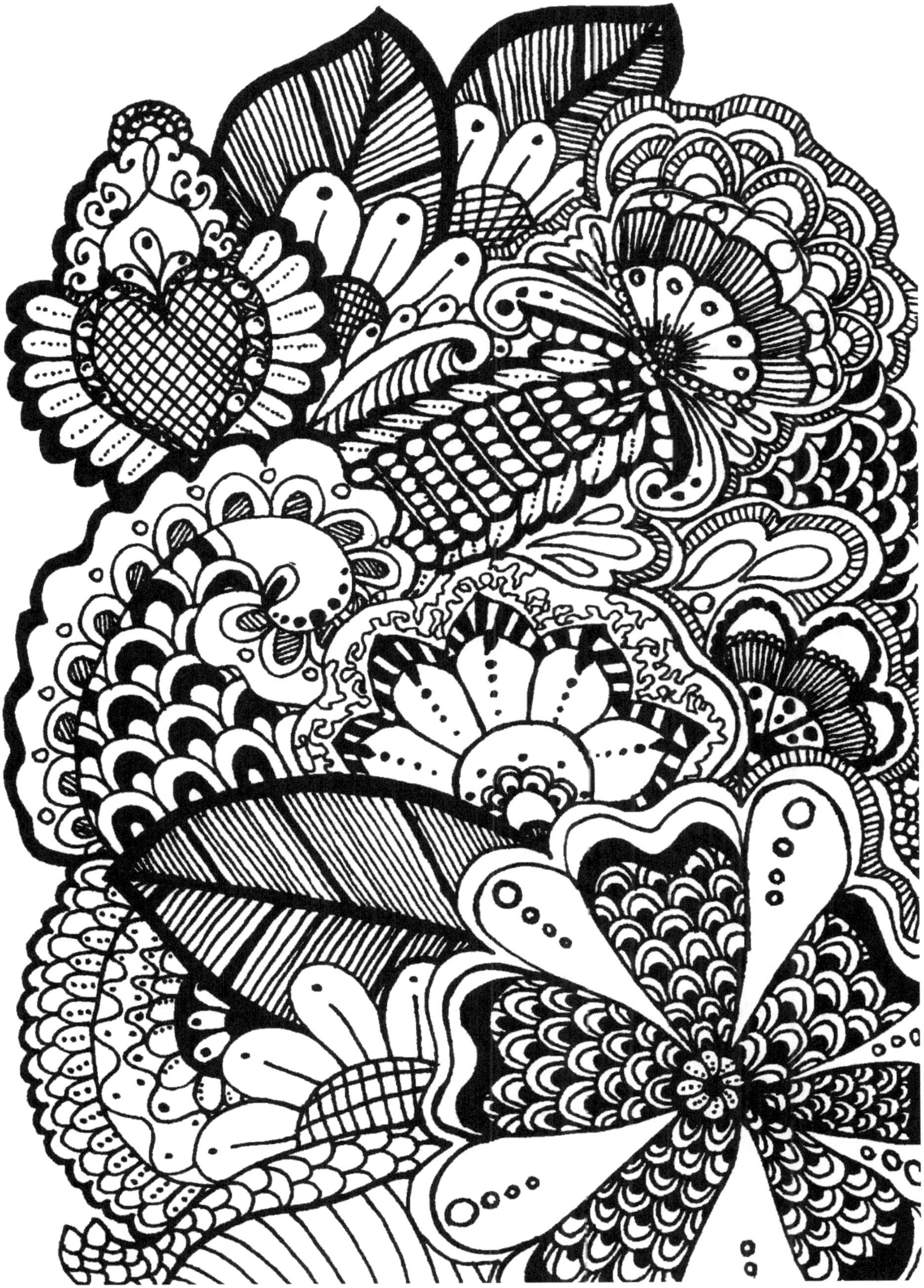

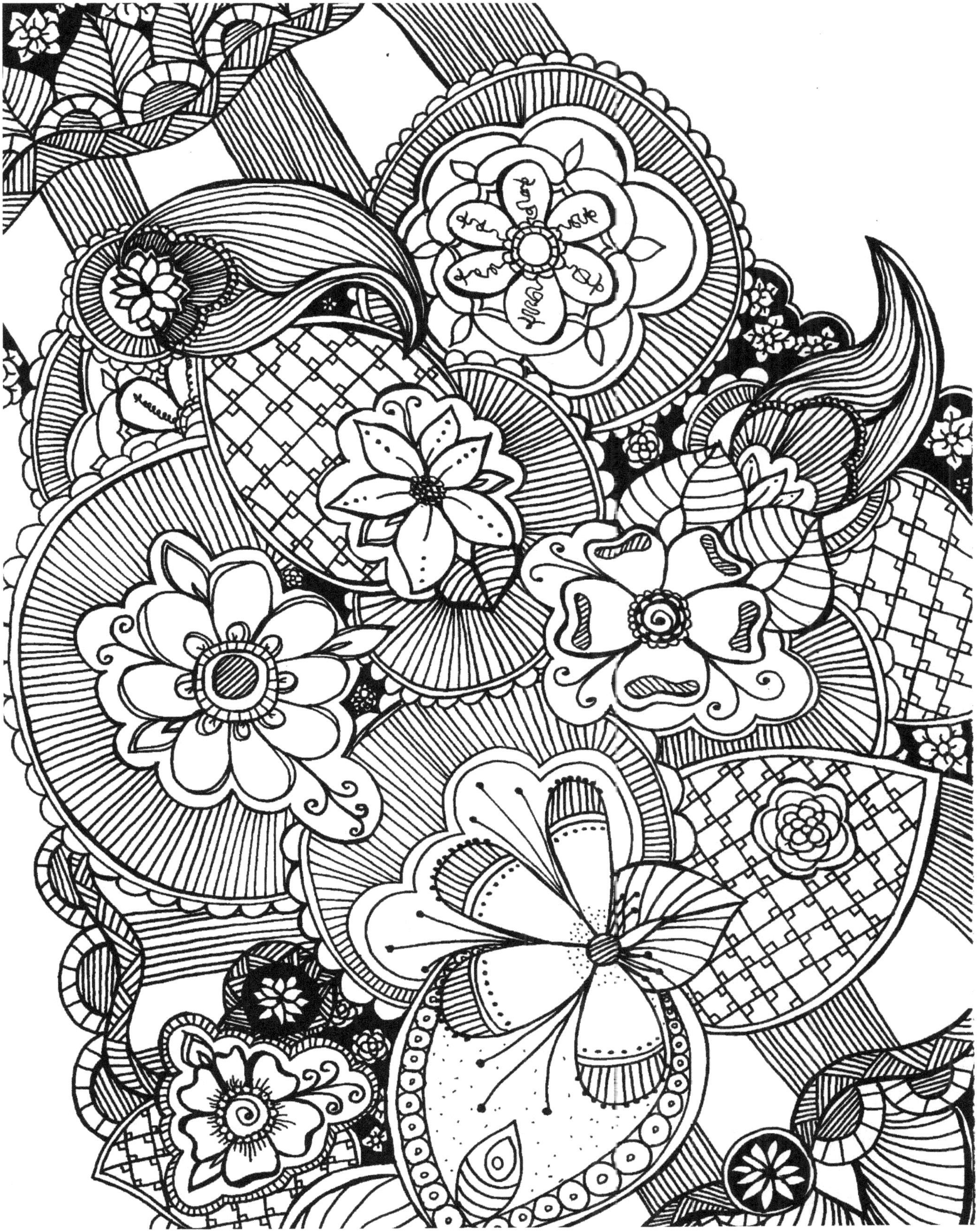

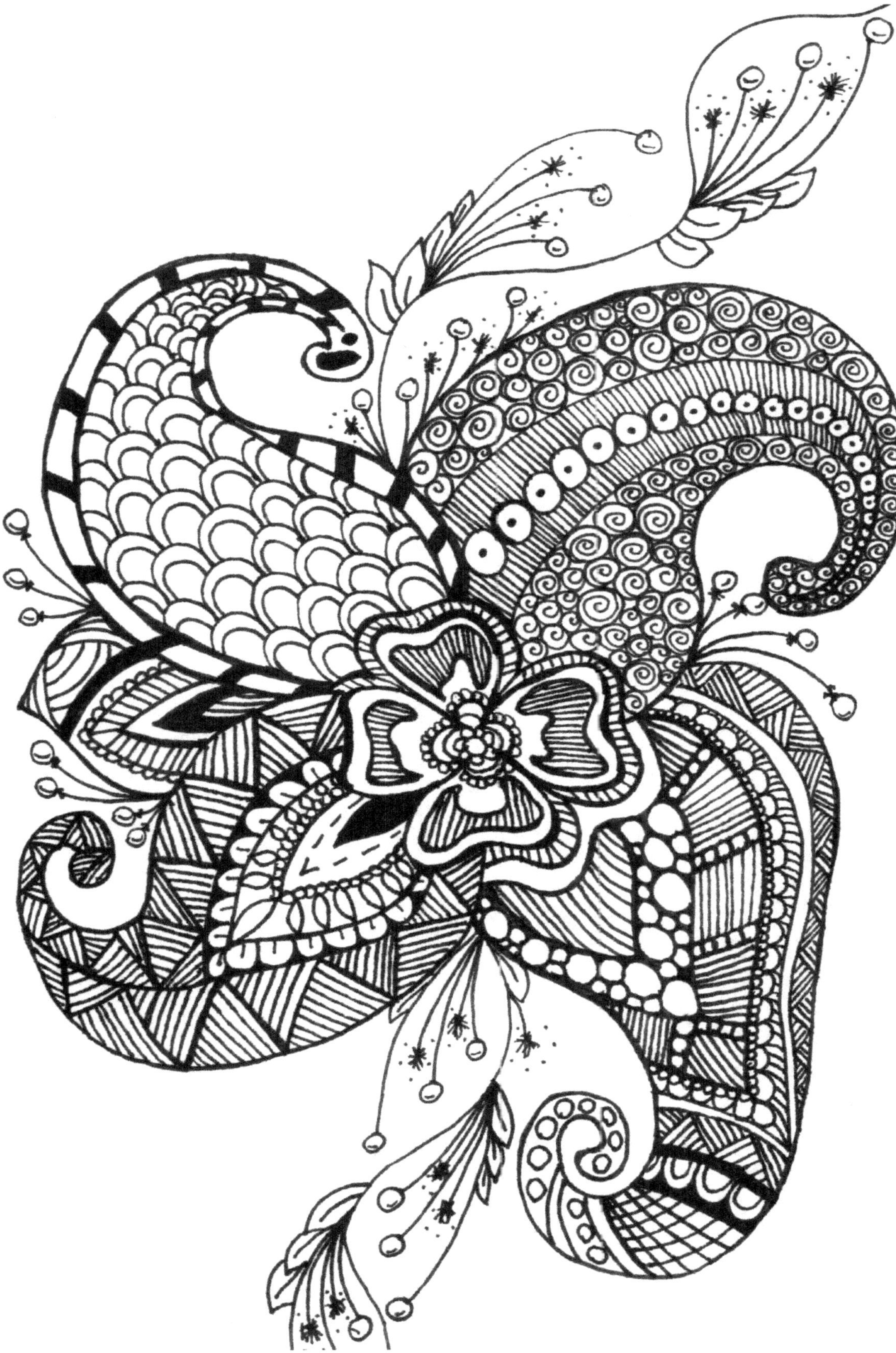

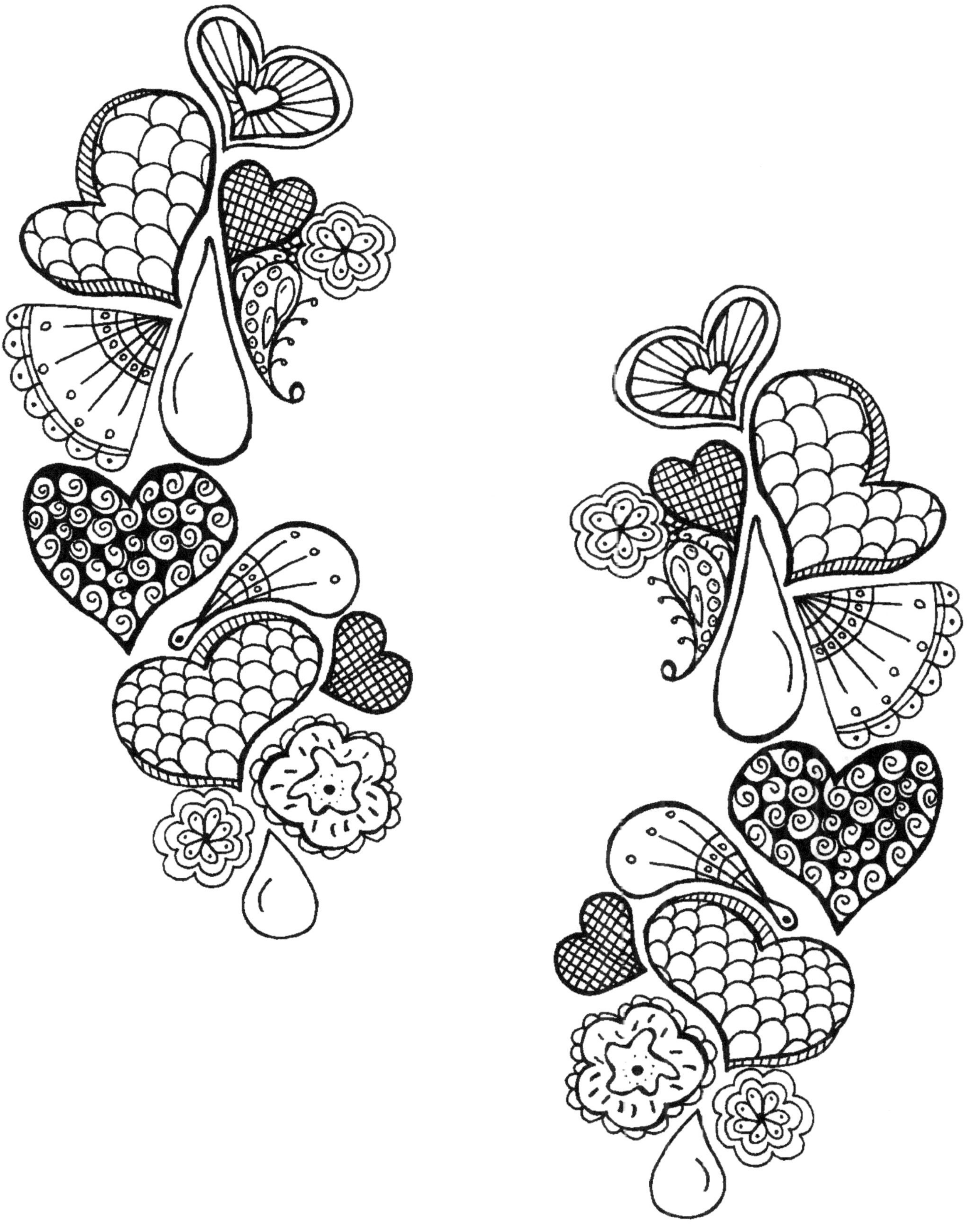

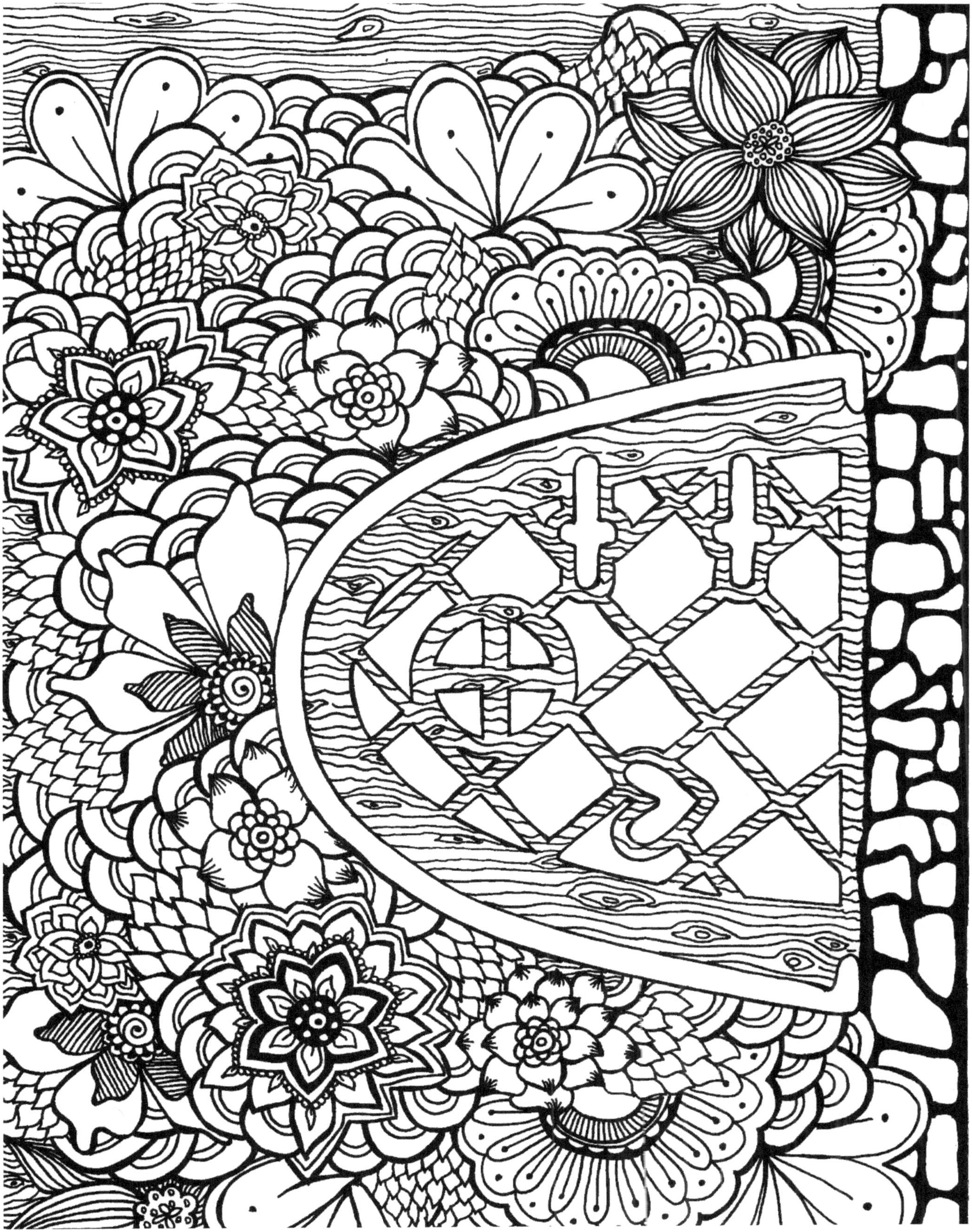

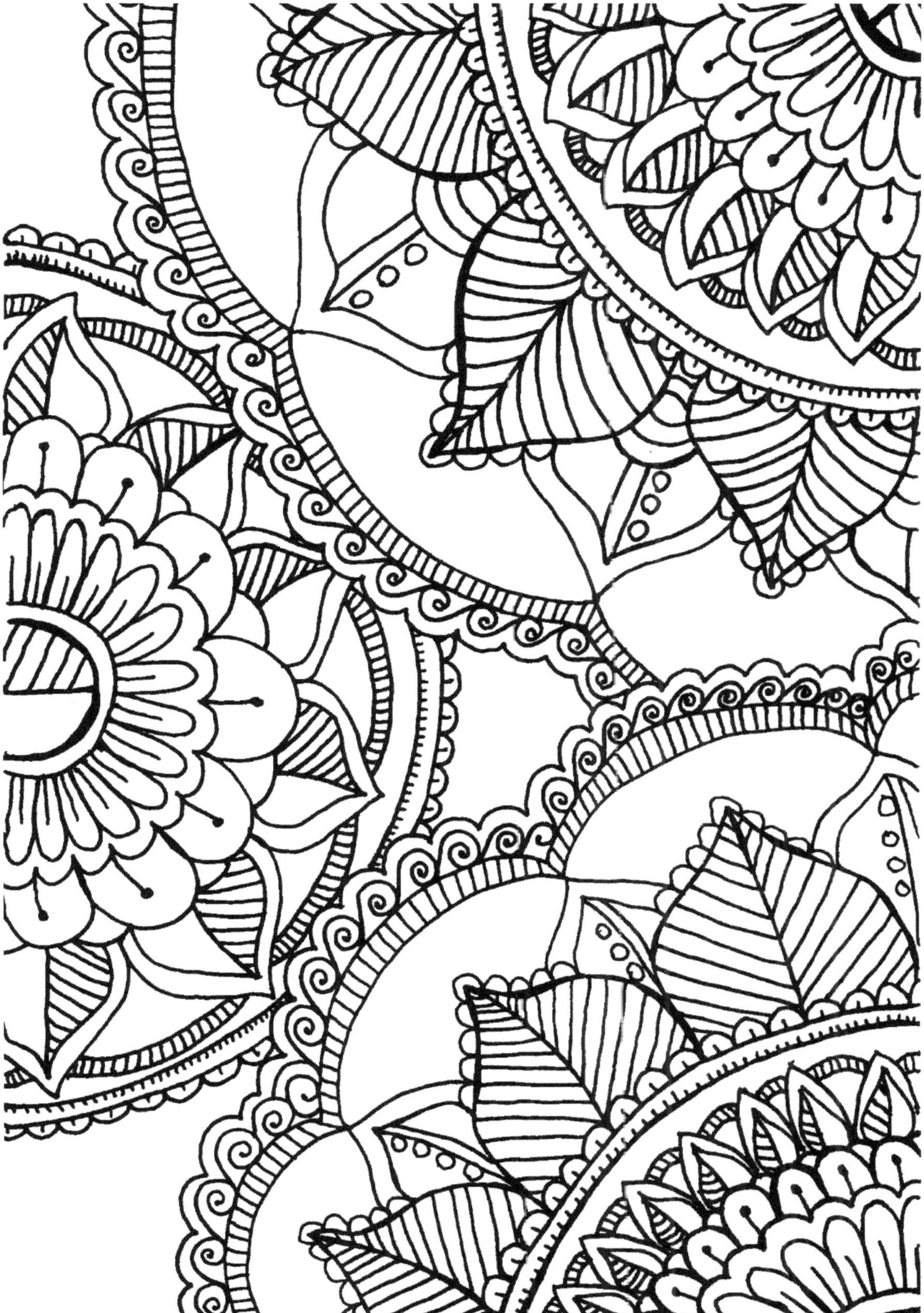

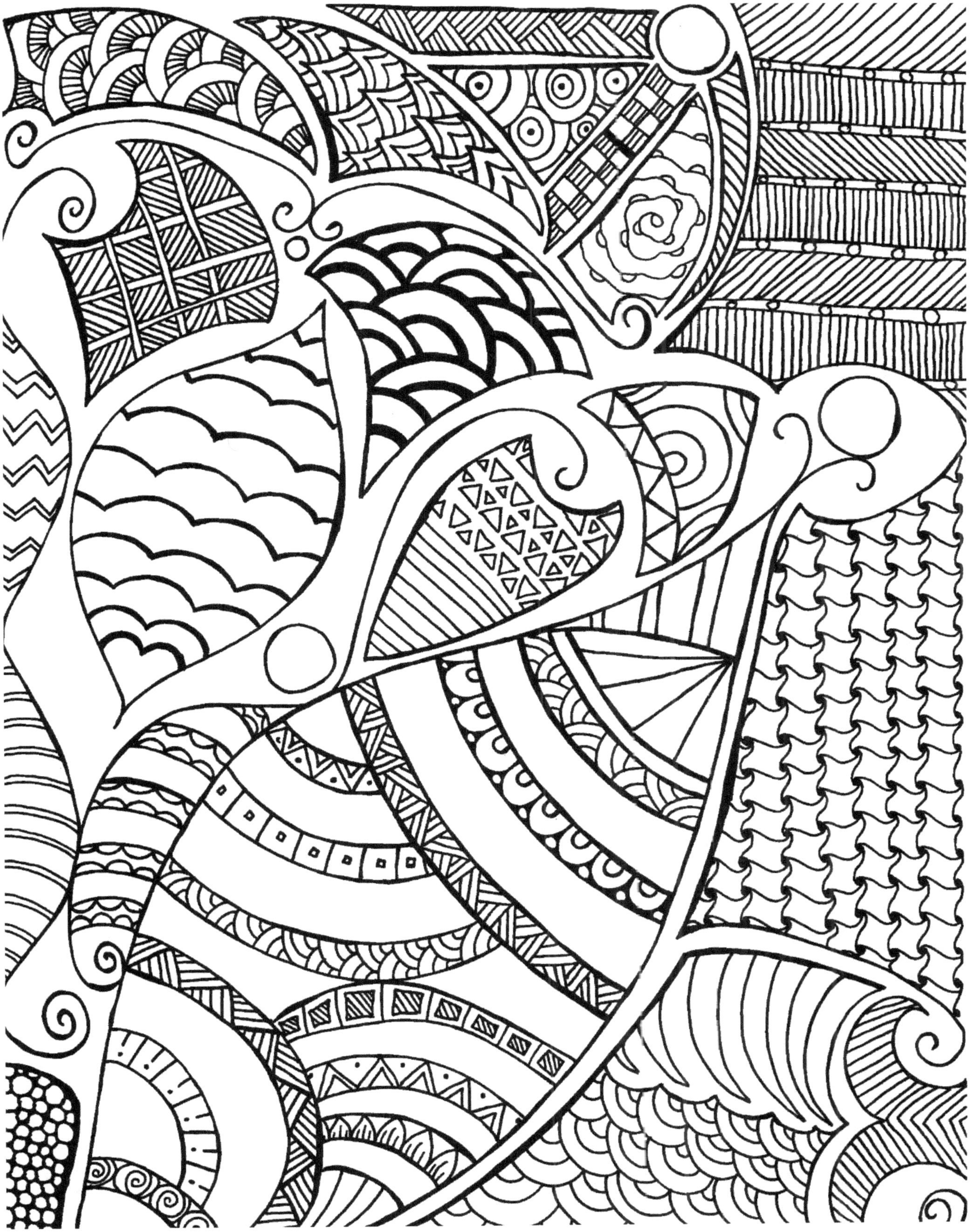

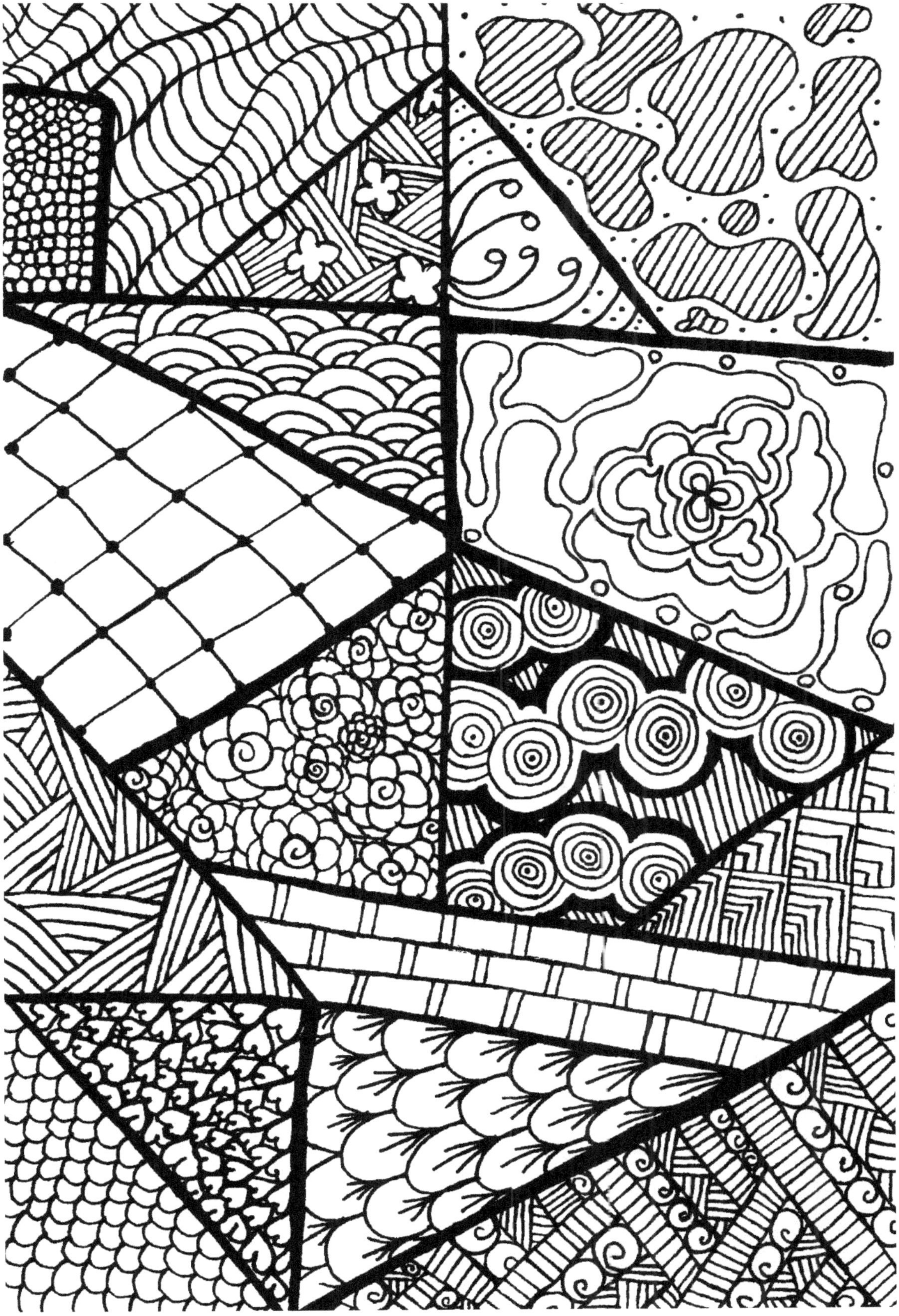

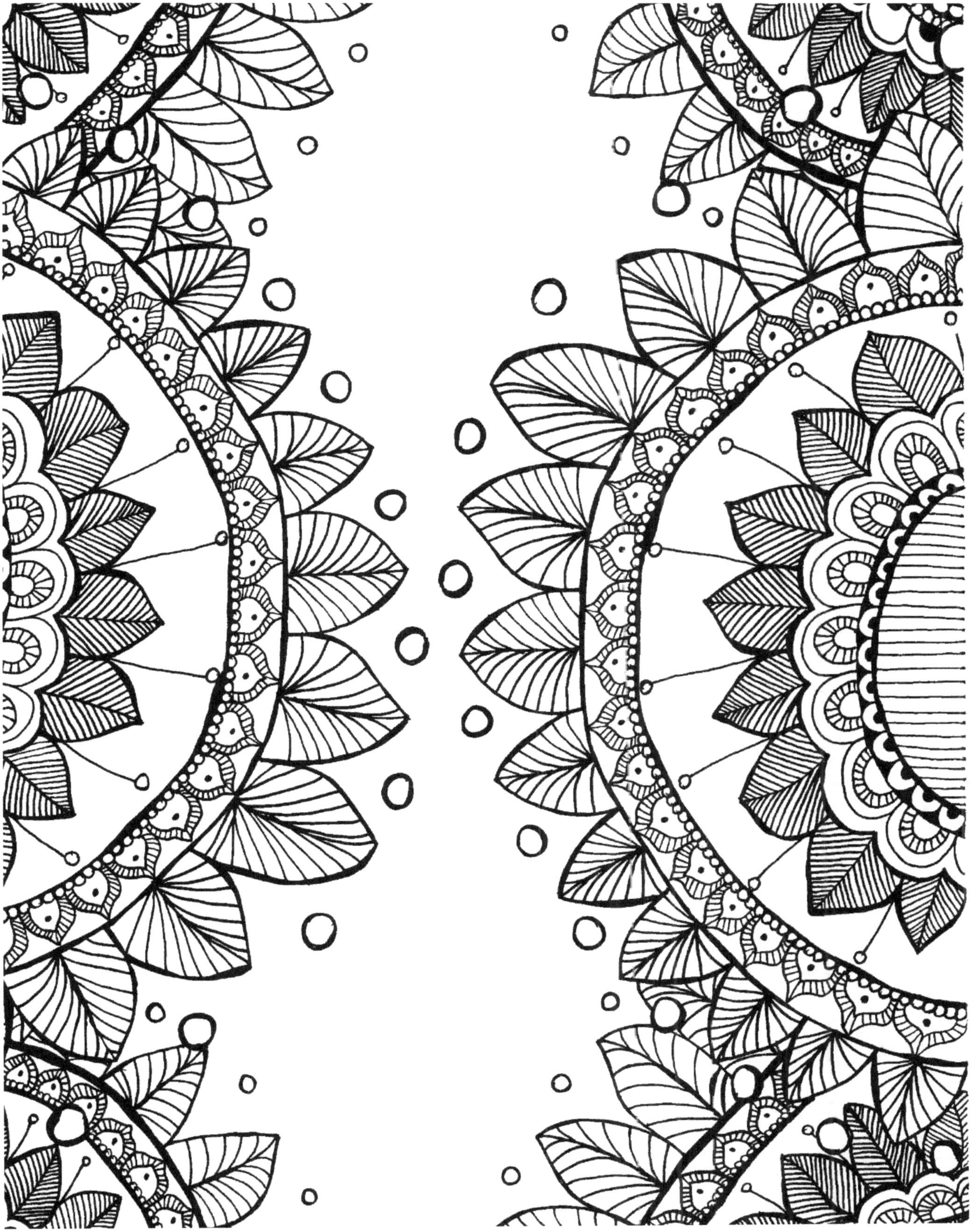

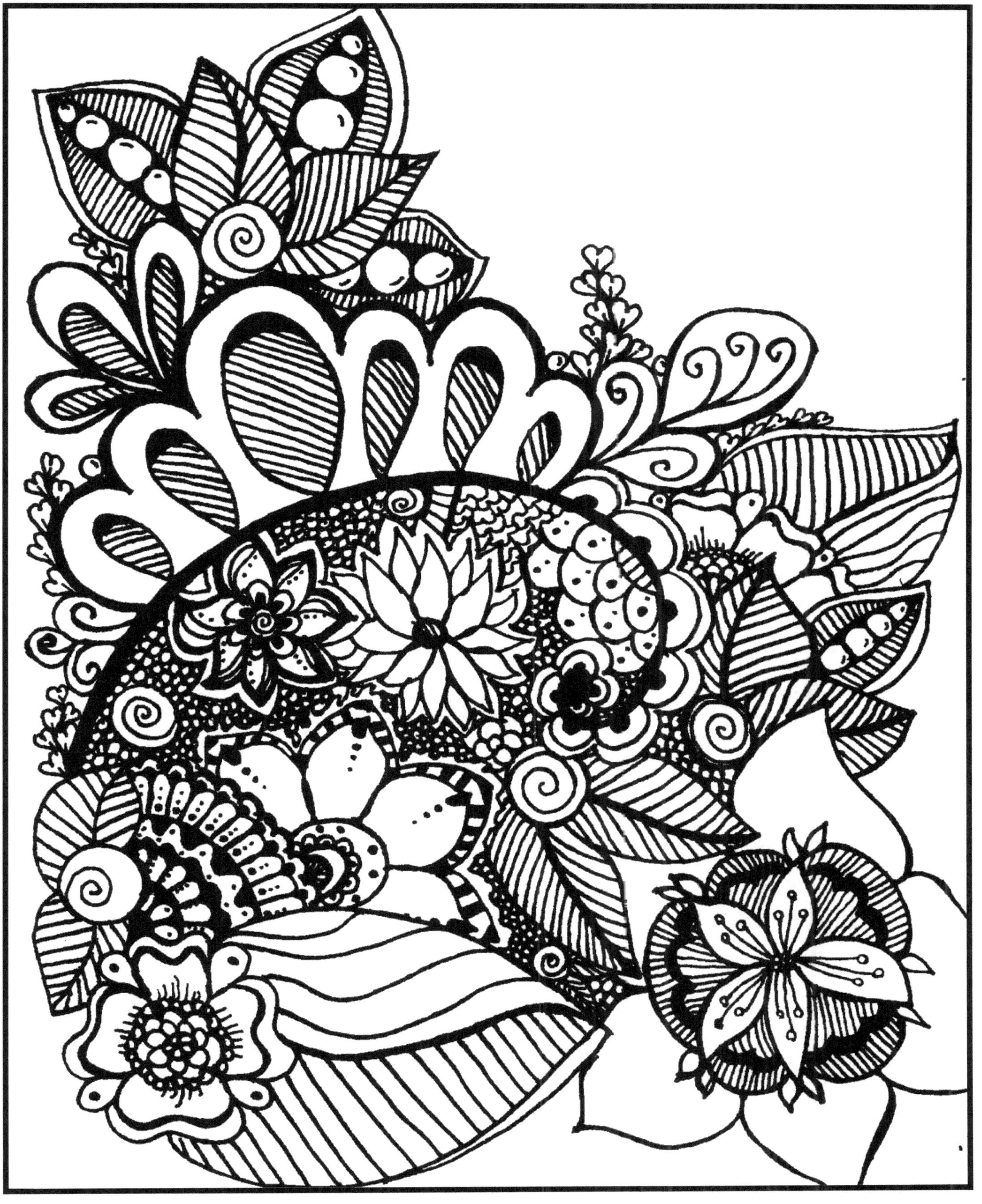

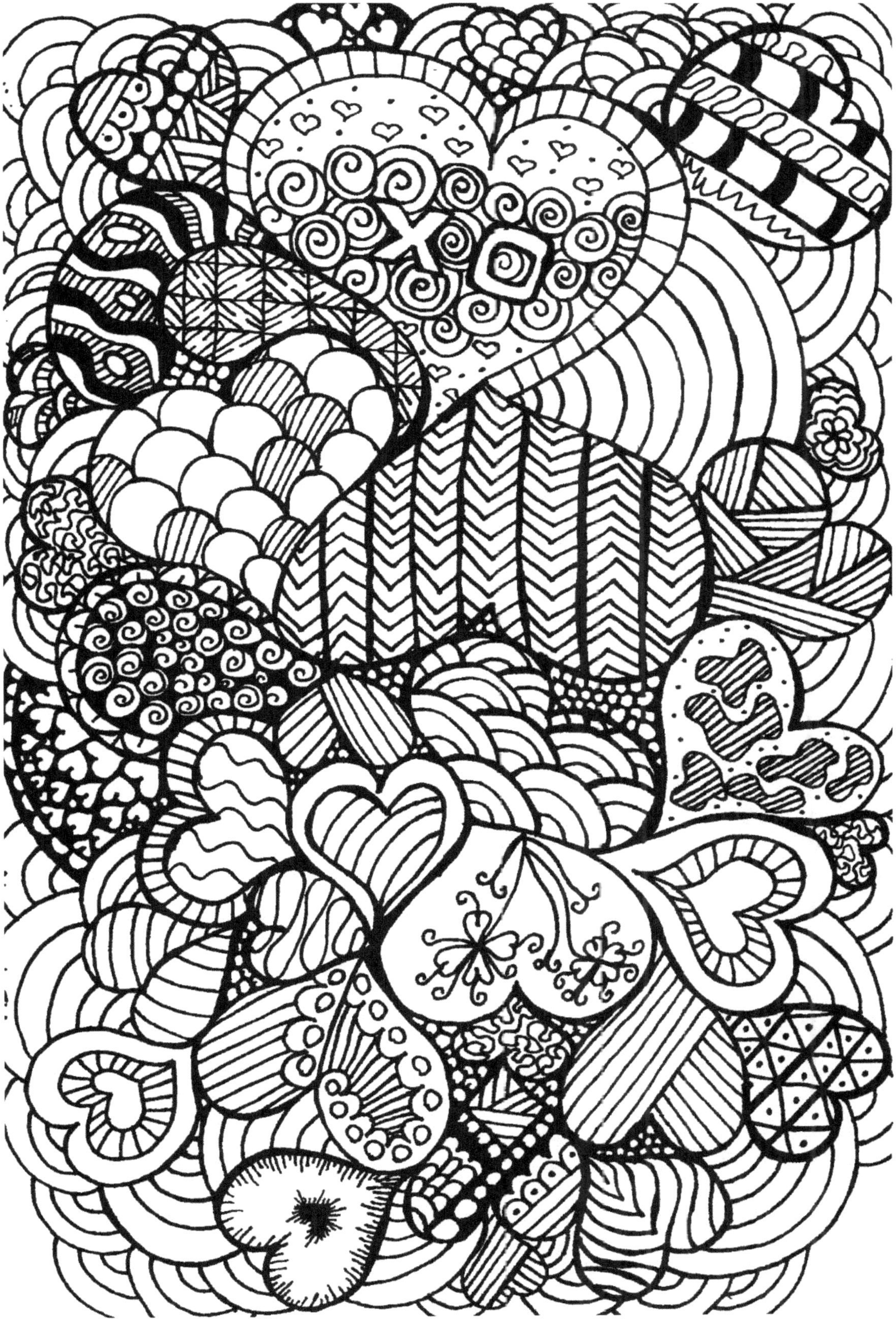

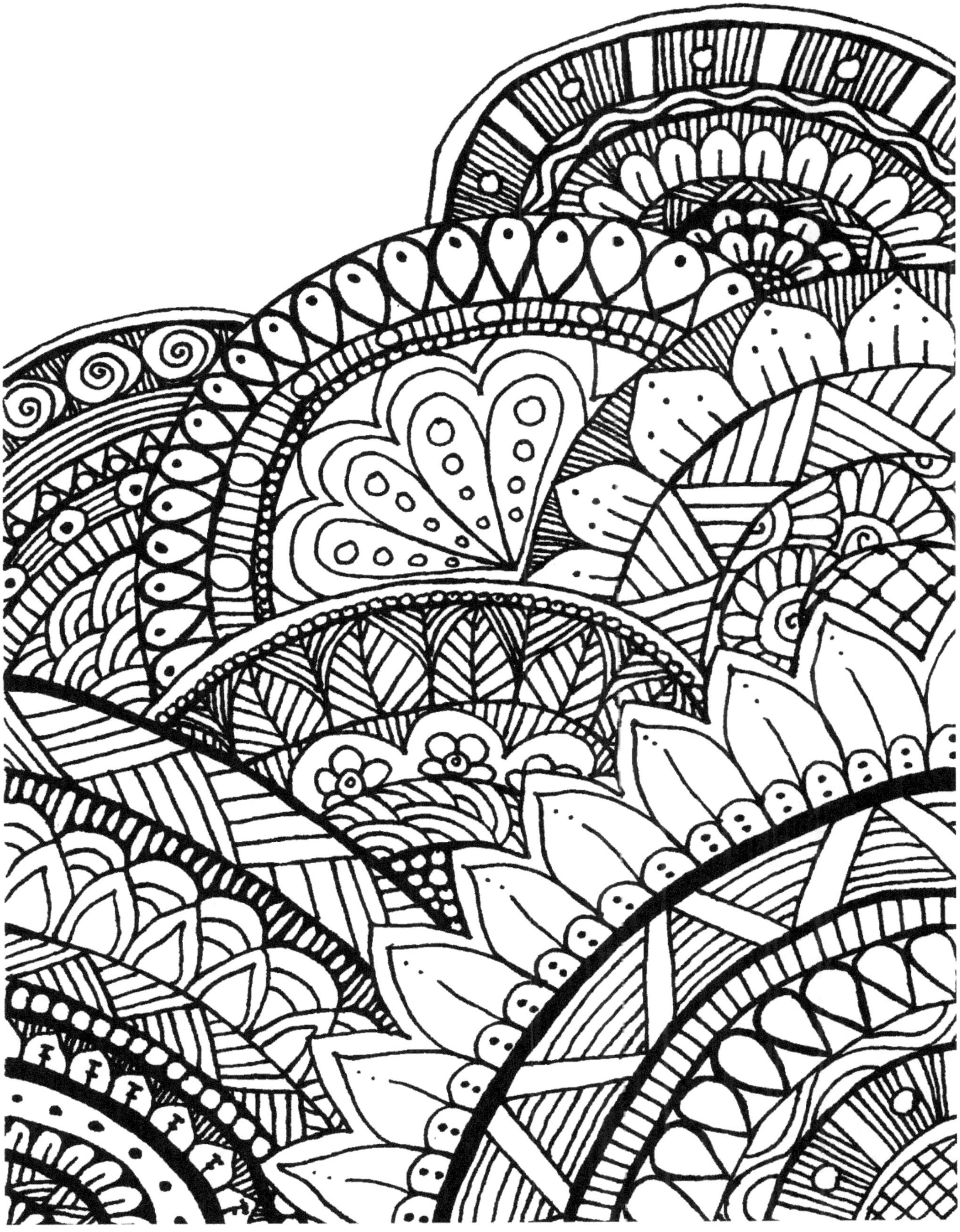

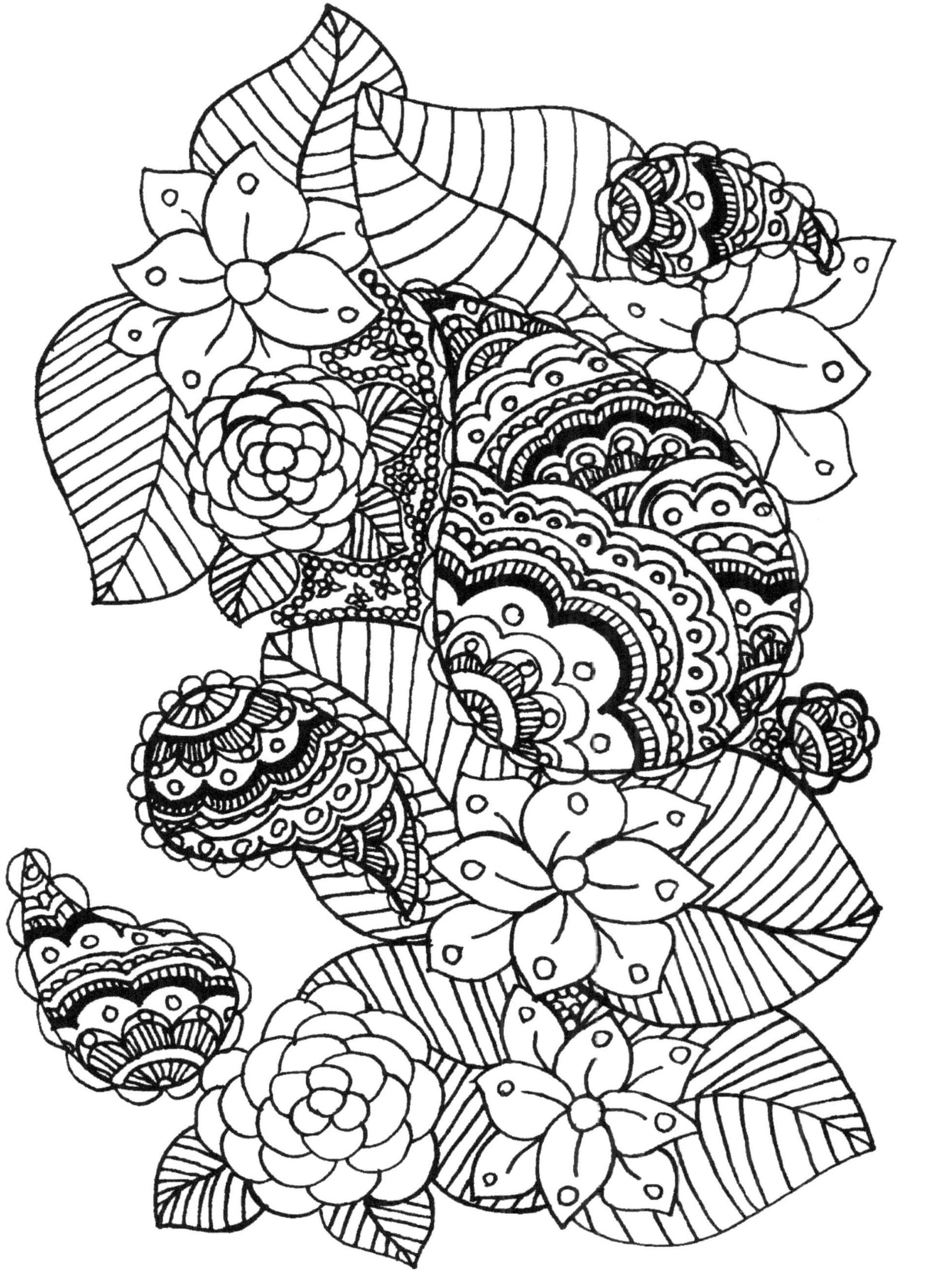

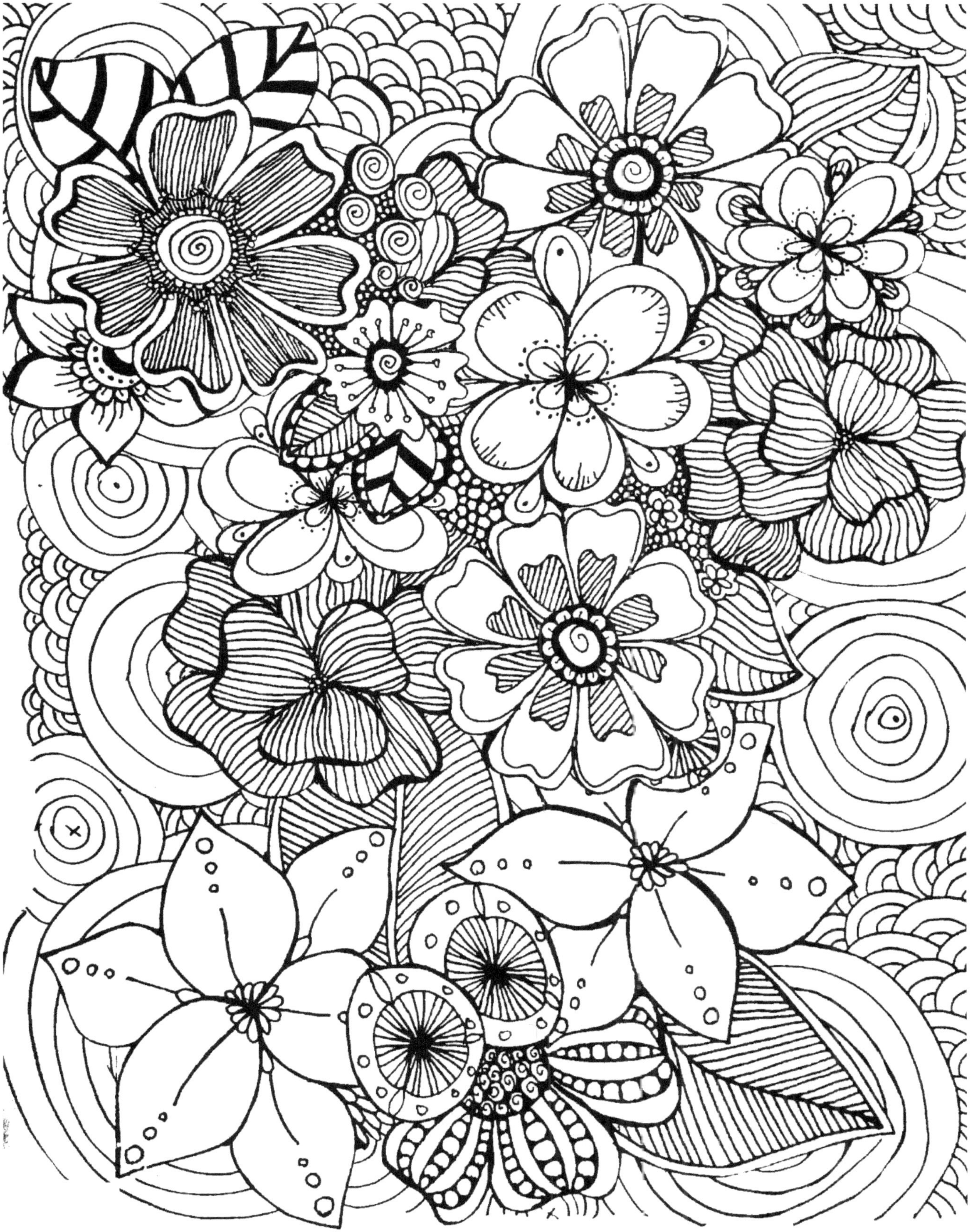

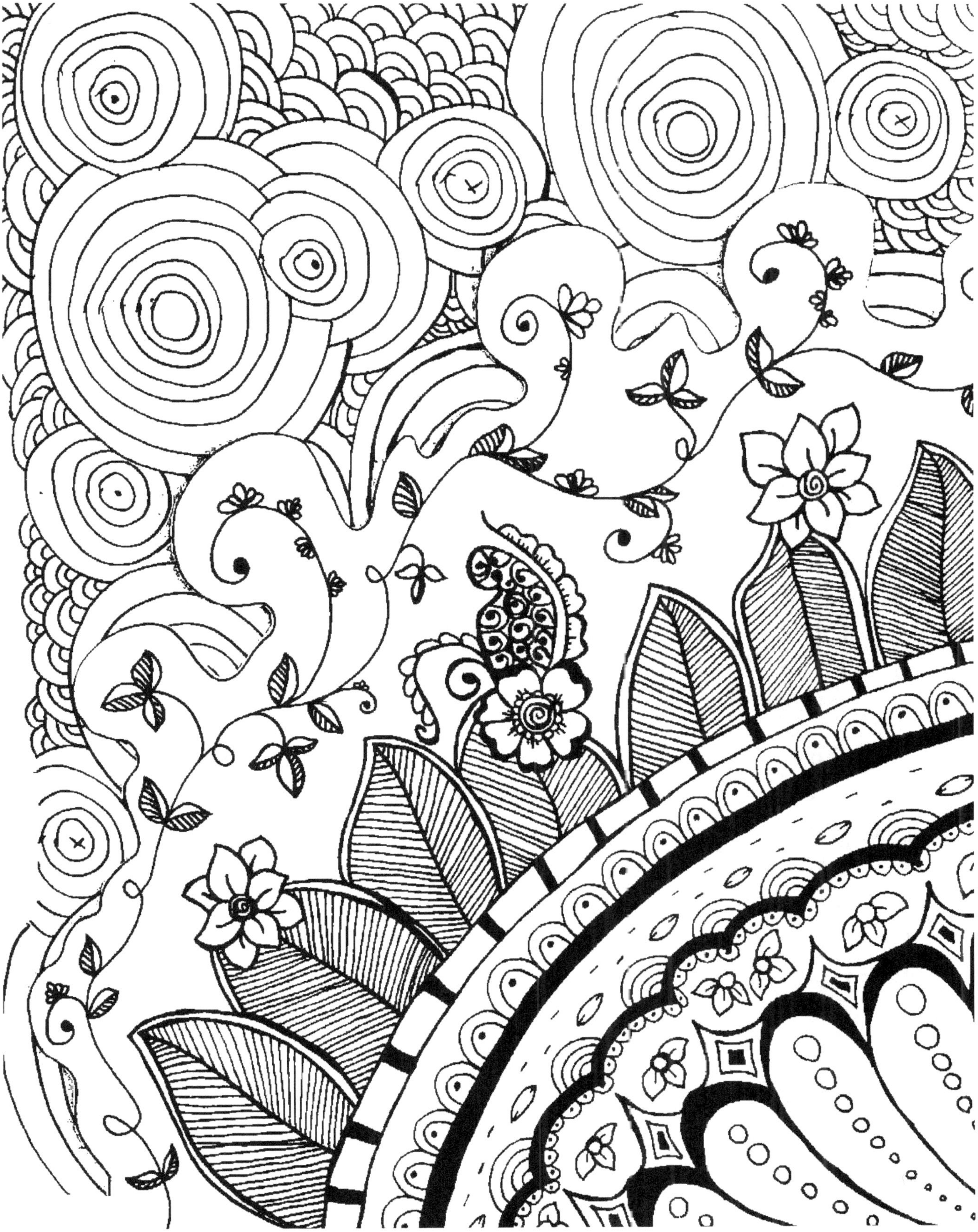

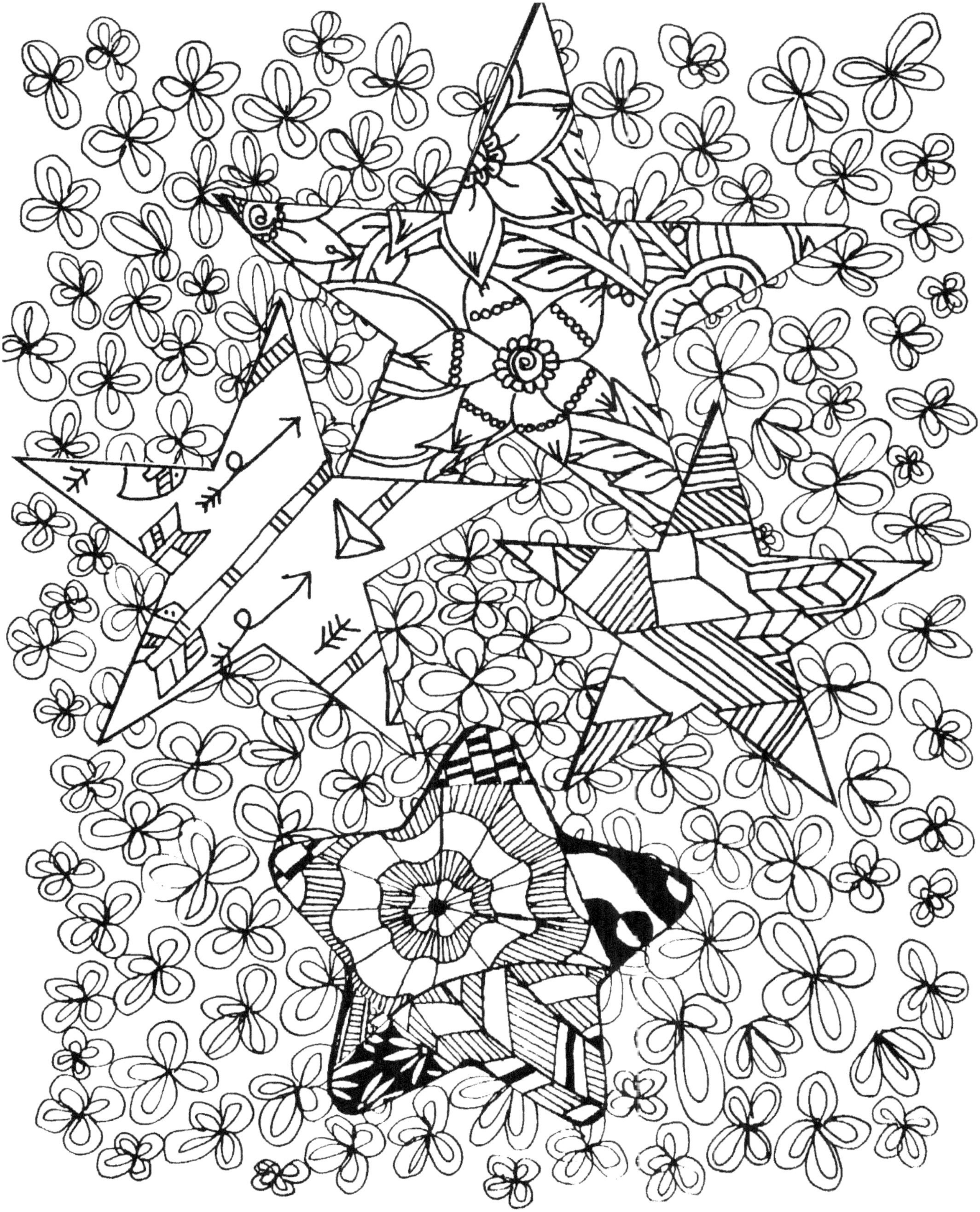

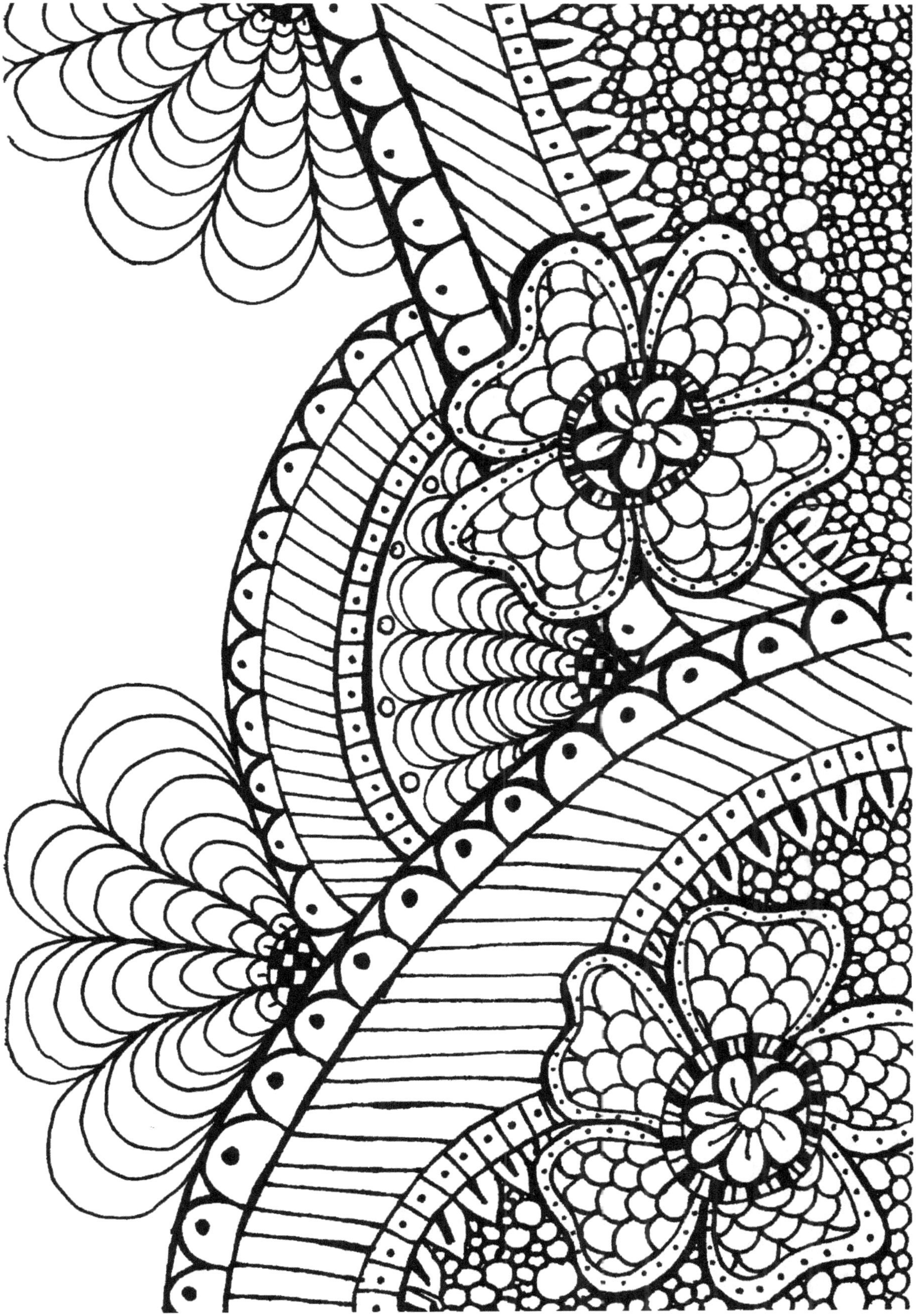

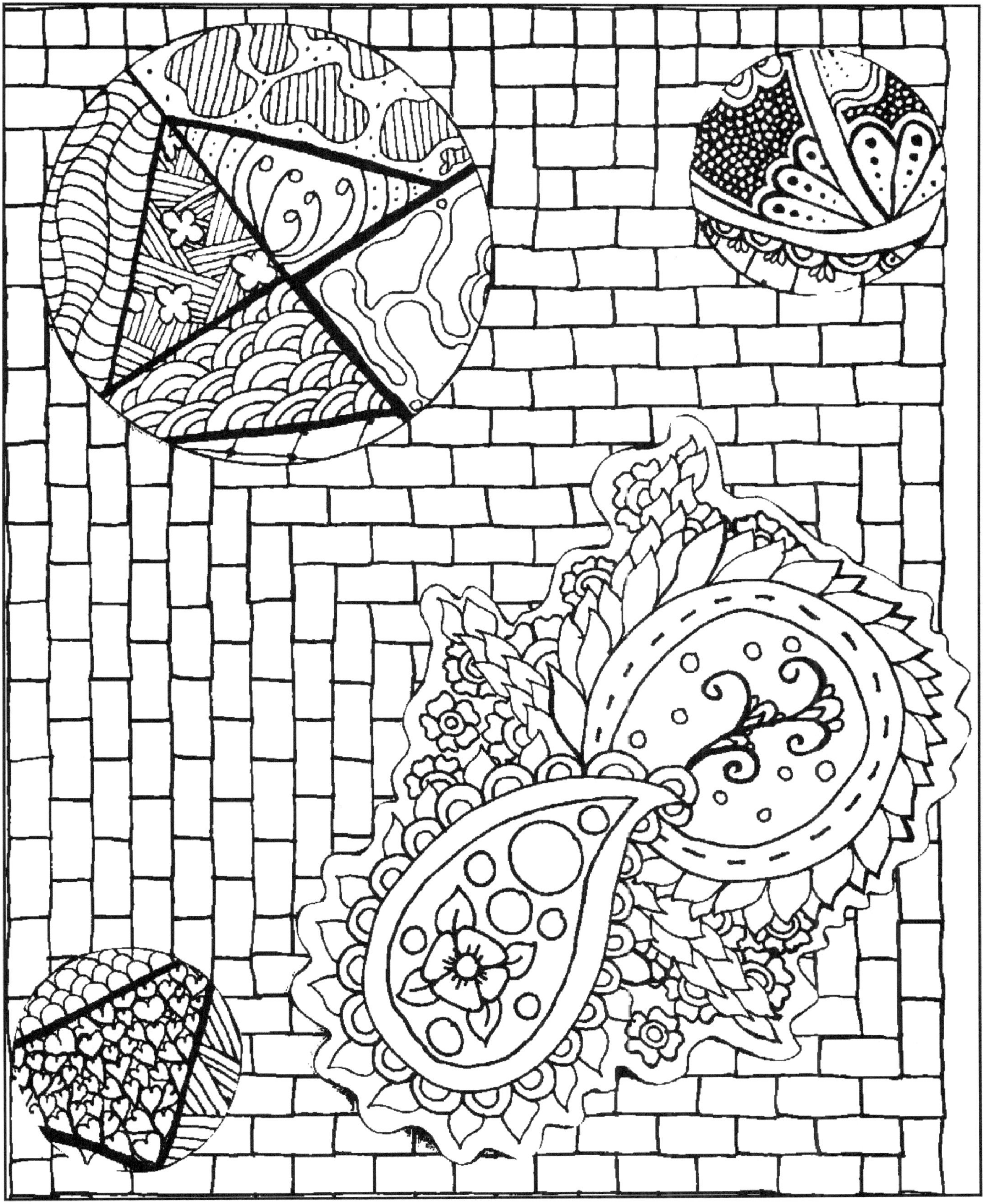

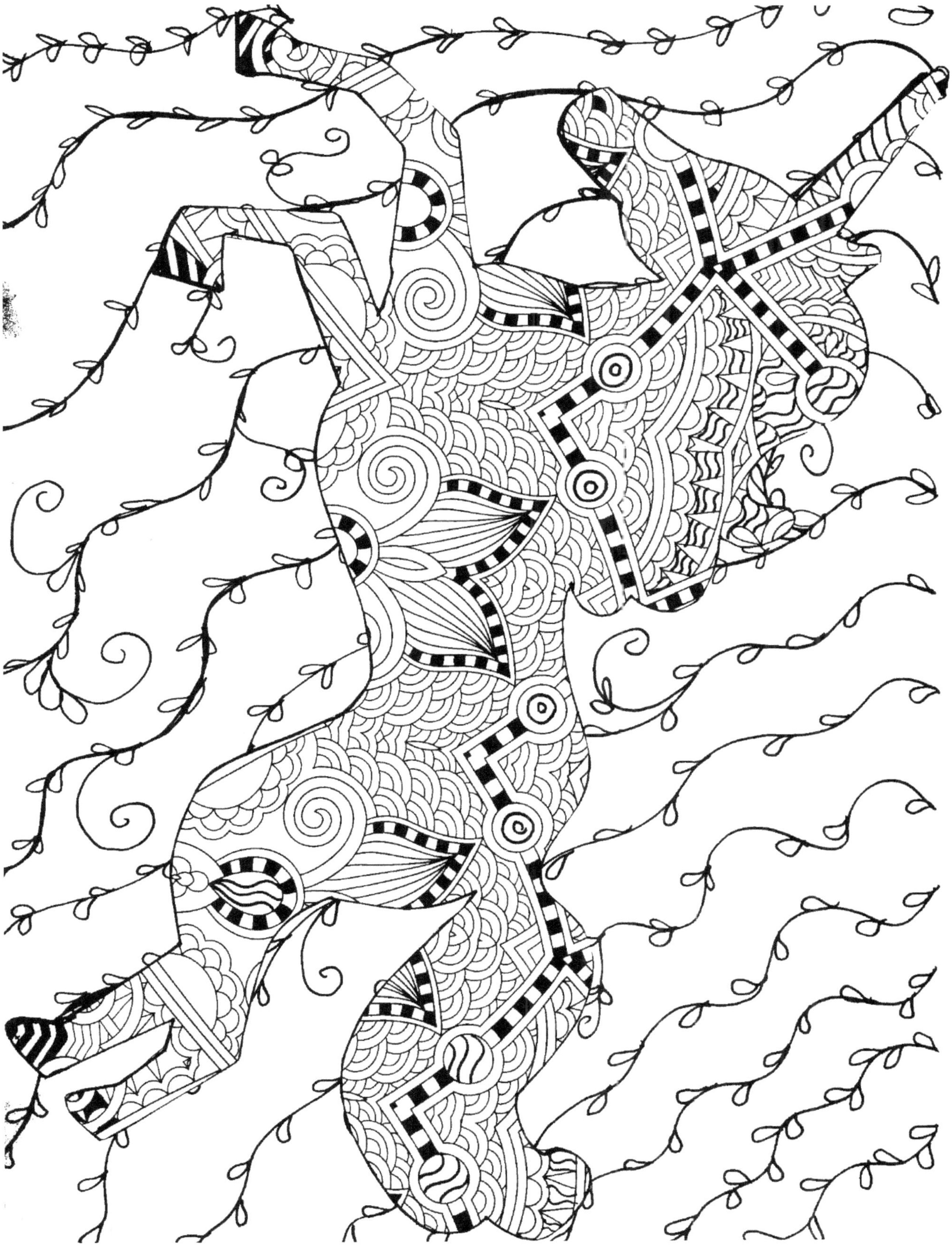

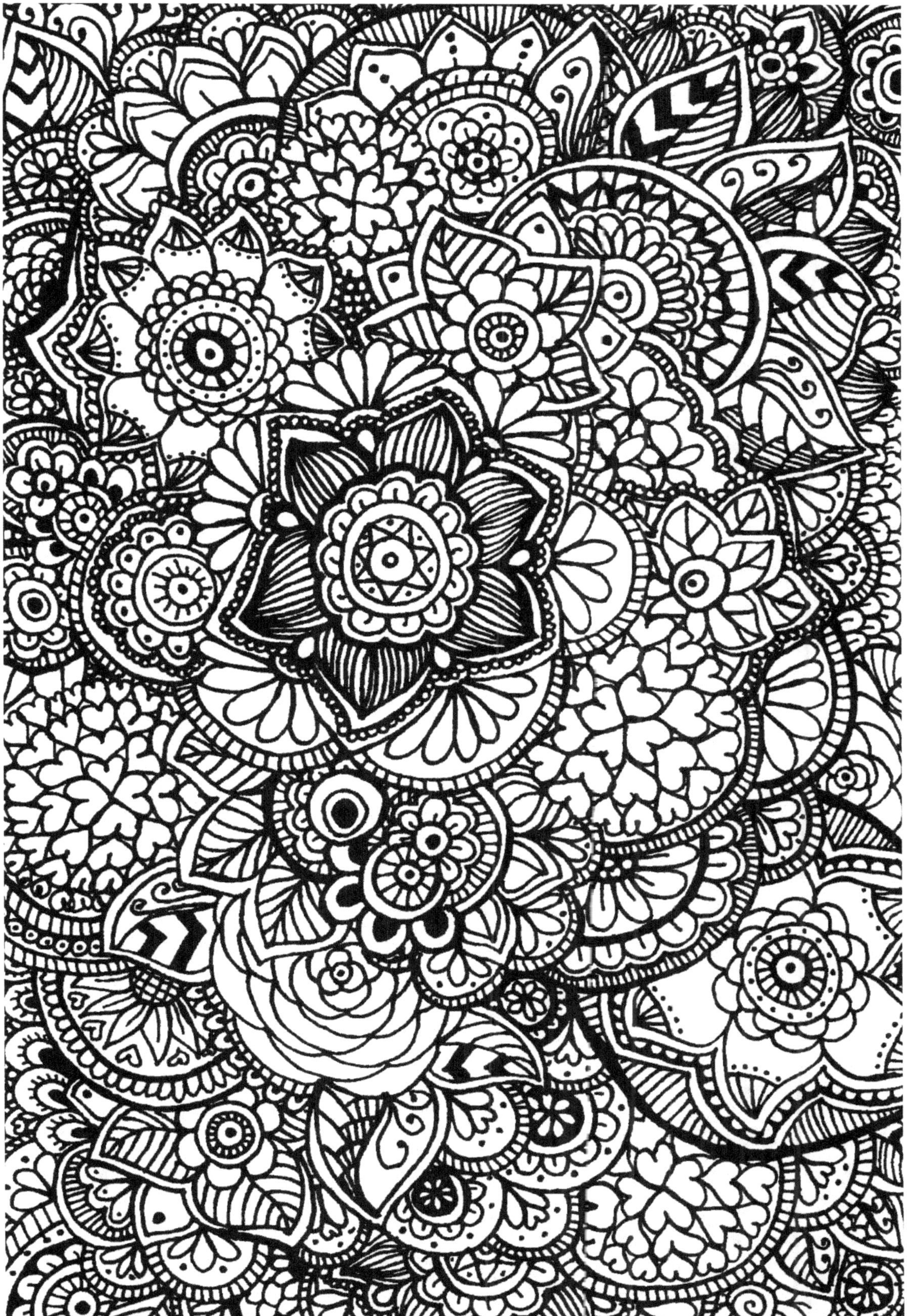

www.ingramcontent.com/pod-product-compliance
Lightning Source LLC
Chambersburg PA
CBHW062125220526
45471CB00010B/3888
* 9 7 8 1 9 8 6 3 0 6 2 4 9 *